# TABLE OF CONTENTS

Page

# MANNING THE U.S. ARMY: MEETING THE MANPOWER GOALS WITH "PEACE BREAKING OUT"

## CHAPTER ONE

## INTRODUCTION

This paper investigates manning the U.S. Army during periods other than mobilization. The focus is on an analysis of the traditional options of the draft, the recruiting of volunteers and the new proposals for a national service corps.

During November 1989, Lieutenant General Allen K. Ono, the Deputy Chief of Staff for Personnel, Headquarters, Department of the Army, made a presentation to the United States Army War College Class of 1990.[1] The major focus of his presentation was the need for a long range personnel plan that will meet the needs of both an expansion and a reduction in the United States Army. He discussed the need for this plan to parallel The Army Plan and the Army planning process. As the Army moves through the 1990's and into the next century, the personnel community will be required to become more responsive to changing national and international security interests - particularly difficult during the current period of uncertainty. To meet this challenge, LTG Ono presented a series of "Operating Principles of Reduction and Expansion" as the framework for the development of the future personnel strategy. The principles, included at Appendix 1, are essentially the same during both an expansion and a reduction environment. With the components of a responsive personnel system in place, the only tasks will be to turn the "knobs" to adjust the flow of accessions.

My concern is that the Army's DCSPER may be taking a traditional approach to a non-traditional problem. Old remedies work well on old illnesses. I believe the challenges of national security in the future represent new challenges and, therefore, require new solutions.

Following all periods of war, the American tradition has been to reduce the size of its army to cadre level. As a nation, we have chosen to rely on mobilization to meet manpower needs when faced with threats to our national security.[2] The period following the Vietnam War is perhaps the one exception. Although not at war, the nation has responded to the threat of the USSR by maintaining a large, forward deployed, standing army. With this one exception, the United States has had a history of expansion, reduction, expansion and then reduction again. The cost has generally been a longer preparation time for war (World War II) or initial ineffectiveness and excessive losses when a period of build up was not available (Korean War).

Unlike previous periods of reduction, it is not the goal of the Army to move to a cadre force. On the contrary, the imperatives for tomorrow's Army call for:

o   A quality force.

o   A dynamic, realistic doctrine.

o   A force mix that meets national security needs.

o   Training that is the cornerstone of readiness.

o   Modernization to keep pace with technology.

o   Leader development.[3]

Adherence to these imperatives will provide an Army that is versatile, deployable and lethal.

In the December 11, 1989 issue of U. S. News & World Report the headline and lead story was "Do we need an Army?". The answer to the question is yes. However, the Army's role may need to be redefined. The good news is the "threat" from the USSR and the Warsaw Pact appears to be on the decline. The bad news is that this "threat" has been the basis of much of the justification for how the U.S. Army has been structured since the end of World War II. So, perhaps if the traditional threat is dissipating, it is reasonable for Congress to give the traditional answer and stand-down the Army and spend the high Department of Defense budget on other national needs.

I think this would be a mistake. Several factors indicate a sizable standing army may be more relevant now than during the past 40 years. These include the existence of regional terrorism, international and domestic drug trafficking, regional instability in parts of the world vital to national interests, and the proliferation of sophisticated weapons in potentially hostile developing nations. Couple these with the United States' role as a world leader and superpower and it is clear there is a need for a viable defense structure and for a viable, capable Army.

By the nature of these new and dangerous challenges, the level of the threat and, therefore, the level of the Army may fluctuate more dramatically and more frequently than it has in the past 20 years. My concern is whether or not the currently planned personnel systems for accession management will be sufficiently responsive to meet the expansion and reduction capability sought by the Army's leaders.

## ENDNOTES

1. Allen K. Ono, LTG, Manning the Force Issues. Cited with special permission of LTG Ono.

2. "There can be no controversy concerning the fear and aversion in the Colonies to what was termed a 'standing army.' The congressional sentiments cited in the memorial to the King were reiterated even more strongly by the Continental Congress in 1784: '...standing armies in time of peace are inconsistent with the principles of republican governments, dangerous to the liberties of a free people, and generally converted into destructive engines for establishing despotism.'" U.S. Department of the Army, Pamphlet No.20-212, p. 3.

3. These are the imperatives of the Army Chief of Staff, General Carl E. Vuono. A more detailed discussion of these imperatives can be found in "Quality Tops Chief's List of Imperatives," Army, December 1989, p. 45.

# CHAPTER TWO

## THE DRAFT

> The draft has been an accepted feature of American life
> for a generation, and its elimination will represent
> still another major change in a society much buffeted
> by change and alarmed by violent attacks on the
> established order. Yet the status quo can be changed
> constructively, and the society improved peacefully, by
> responsible and responsive government. It is in this
> spirit that the Commission has deliberated and arrived
> at its recommendations. However necessary conscription
> may have been in World War II, it has revealed many
> disadvantages in the past generation. The draft has
> been a costly, inequitable, and divisive procedure for
> recruiting men for the armed forces. It has imposed
> heavy burdens on a small minority of young men while
> easing slightly the tax burden on the rest of us. It
> has introduced needless uncertainty into the lives of
> all our young men. It has burdened draft boards with
> painful decisions about who shall be compelled to serve
> and who shall be deferred. It has weakened the
> political fabric of our society and impaired the
> delicate web of shared values that alone enables a free
> society to exist.[1]

The President's Commission on the All-Volunteer Armed Force,

which convened in March 1969, had as its goal to develop a

comprehensive plan for eliminating conscription and to move

toward an all-volunteer armed force. The Commission, also known

as the Gates Commission, achieved its goal. The Commission

concluded that the all-volunteer force could meet United States

security requirements and that the draft should be established as

a standby system by 30 June 1971.[2]

The President accepted the recommendations of the Gate's

Commission, Congress amended the Selective Service Act and the

Department of Defense issued the last draft calls in December 1972.

As the nation moves through another phase of national security during the 1990's, a reexamination of the draft and of its potential role in manning the armed forces is in order. In particular, a look at the usefulness of the draft to the Army is needed.

## BACKGROUND

The United States of America has been involved in five wars that were declared by Congress: the War of 1812, the Mexican War (1846-1848), the Spanish-American War (1898), World War I (1917-1918), and World War II (1941-1945). The Civil War (1861-1866), the Korean Conflict (1950-1953) and the Vietnam Conflict (1957-1975) were never formally declared by Congress.[3]

We have been a nation that relied on a militia system for defense. Prior to the Revolutionary War, the colonists relied on this system to meet manpower needs. Once the Revolutionary War started, some states were forced to resort to a draft to meet quotas that were established by the Continental Congress.[4] A drawing by lot from all eligible men was the typical system used. This laid the groundwork for the use of a system of impartiality, selection by lot, which persisted through the 1970's.

The draft was used extensively to provide manpower in two of the declared wars: World War I and World War II. Conscription was also used during the Civil War, the Korean Conflict and the

Vietnam Conflict. In these wars, Congress enacted draft legislation that stipulated "...our nati. al ideal of freedom...is based on the premise that individual and national liberty is enhanced, rather than destroyed, by compelling military service for defense of the nation."[5]

After World War II, the strength of the armed forces dwindled below a level desired by the Department of Defense (1.4 million versus 2 million) and Congress enacted the Selective Service Act of 1948. This marked the first time in our nation's history that Americans were drafted in peacetime. Some 300,000 men were drafted under the 1948 Act. Most of these men served only twelve of the twenty-one month obligation. The Act was up for renewal in June 1950 when the North Korean Communists invaded South Korea. The Selective Service Act of 1948 was extended until July 1951 when it was succeeded by the Universal Military and Training Act.[6]

More than 1.5 million men were inducted into the armed forces during the Korean Conflict.[7] The Universal Military and Training Act was extended until 1959 and for the first time added deferments for college students and for "essential service to the nation" employment to the traditional marriage deferments. The Act continued to be renewed through 1964.

The Act provided inductees throughout the Vietnam War. The general unpopularity of that war, coupled with the militancy of college students brought conscription under heavy fire. Reviews of the Selective Service System by Presidents Johnson and Nixon led to its expiration, as mentioned in the beginning of this chapter.

Was the draft vital to our national defense capability?

Historically, the draft has not provided the bulk of the armed forces - with the exception of the two world wars:

| PERIOD | % OF FORCE DRAFTED |
|---|---|
| Civil War (1865) | 2 |
| Spanish-American War (1898) | 0 |
| World War I | 59 |
| World War II | 61 |
| Korean Conflict | 27 |
| 1960 | 15 |
| 1965 | 16[8] |

The data can suggest that conscription is not necessarily required for conflicts comparable in scale to those fought since World War II.

> The maximum active duty force levels reached during the Korean and Vietnamese Wars were 3.7 million and 3.6 million respectively. The Korean War force represented 15 percent of the male population age 18 to 39 in 1952, and the Vietnam War force represented 12.4 percent of the male population age 18 to 39 in 1968. In prosecuting those wars with conscripts, the nation imposed a heavy tax on a small segment of the population. In all, 5.8 million men saw service during the Korean War and 6.0 million during the Vietnam War. In neither case was a serious attempt made to expand the forces with volunteers, and in the Vietnam War little use was made of the Reserves.[9]

Today, a Standby Draft system is in place. Males, at age 18, are required to register for the draft. The question is, do these manpower pools represent a viable resource to meet the "Operating Principles of Reduction and Expansion" as outlined by LTG Ono?

# ASSESSMENT

The report of the Gate's Commission and countless other
sources provide an analysis of the deficiencies of the draft.
The consensus is that the draft is unfair and politically
dangerous.

**UNFAIR IN ITS LACK OF UNIVERSALITY.** Not all of the
available population is needed to meet the manpower needs of the
armed forces. In 1989, only one of every nineteen qualified
males, between the ages of eighteen and twenty-four, were
required to meet the services recruiting goals.[10] The "Why
me?" for the citizen selected by a cleanly run lottery is
difficult to answer. It gets even more difficult if the manpower
needs continue to be reduced in the coming decade as is currently
planned.

Universality goes beyond the unconstrained probability of
selection. It is also the measure of eligibility and how that is
defined. When deferments are granted, additional "haves and have
nots" are created. Then the armed forces does not get a cross
section of American youth. It is more likely to get a very
narrow part of the population which cannot afford the deferments.

**UNFAIR IN ITS EXCLUSION OF WOMEN.** This is also a
universality issue, but it is deserving of separate attention.
For a dozen or more years, the role of women in the Armed Forces
has been debated. The Army has attempted to fully integrate

women into all career fields and remain consistent with the Combat Exclusion Policy and Direct Combat Probability Coding. Sparked by varying reports on the participation of women soldiers in "Operation Just Cause" in Panama in December 1989, new discussions by Members of Congress and the Defense Advisory Committee on Women in the Services (DACOWITS) have challenged the legitimacy of the Army's policy and of the Air Force's and the Navy's statutory limits on the role of women. As these discussions continue, the fairness of denying women the opportunity to be drafted should also be addressed. From the perspective of fairness, the "Why me?" male conscript may ask that women be eligible to be involuntarily drafted. Many women are seeking to be entitled to volunteer with men, under the concept of equality, for any career field for which they are mentally and physically qualified. The same concept of equality should also apply to the draft.

**UNFAIR IN ITS ENFORCEMENT.** The courts have repeatedly upheld the constitutionality of conscripted service for the defense of the nation. Unfortunately, the citizenry has not traditionally been unanimous in embracing the ideal and the nobility of such service. The result is a halfhearted enforcement of the registration law and, during periods of the use of conscription in unpopular wars, inconsistent enforcement standards by various courts and judges.

**UNFAIR AS A TAX.** For the conscripted, a penalty accrues, which the Gate's Commission referred to as a "tax". This "tax" takes several forms. First, the conscript is required to provide a service not required of all the citizens - a levy not paid by all.  Second, the unwilling conscript is paid less than his potential in other occupations and typically less than the volunteer serviceman.[11]  The Gate's Commission concluded:

> The fact that conscription imposes a tax is not in itself immoral and undesirable.  Taxes are required to enable government to exist.  What is of questionable morality is the discriminatory form that this implicit tax takes; and even more, the abridgement of individual freedom that is involved in collecting it...The tax is discriminatory because the first-term servicemen who pay it constitute a small portion of the total population.[12]

**POLITICALLY DANGEROUS.**  Perhaps, more than any other reason, the use of the draft ended due to the political pressures on Presidents Johnson and Nixon caused by the unpopularity of the Vietnam War.  Conscription has never been a popular idea - even during wars when overwhelming national support existed.  When a political decision-maker has an alternative, the politically advantageous choice will usually be taken.


**ANOTHER VIEW**

John Kester in "The Reasons to Draft", a paper written for publication in <u>The All-Volunteer Force After a Decade</u>, presents a series of arguments defending a draft that would serve the country better than an all-volunteer force.[13]  He advocates a "... selective draft of mentally and physically qualified young male Americans...with few exceptions and few deferments...for active duty of, say, fifteen months...to make up the short fall

of qualified volunteers."[14]  Mr. Kester argues from a
perspective of a "sounder social policy".

The gist of his arguments focus on:

**EQUITY.**  He believes that the middle class and most of the
fortunate of society would be available if deferments were
properly managed.

**MILITARY EXPERIENCE.**  He says that broadening the military
experience in society has the effect of keeping the military from
becoming a "foreign world" to its citizens.  Practical experience
enables society to have a knowledge that goes beyond Hollywood's
movie imagination - a particularly pointed issue as it applies to
Congressional decision making.

**ALLIES.**  Pointing out that NATO allies have questioned the
United States' seriousness of purpose since the abolishment of
conscription, he notes that military service and conscription are
standards for most all young men in the other NATO nations.

**MOBILIZATION.**  Clearly, he states, all agree that volunteers
alone cannot meet all the manpower needs generated during a
protracted war or a national emergency requiring rapid
acquisition of large numbers of recruits.

**COSTS.**  He theorizes that conscripts are cheaper for the
American tax payer.  Mr. Kester points out they do not cost as
much to recruit and that they can generally be paid less than the
volunteers.[15]

Mr. Kester concludes his arguments by stating:

> I realize that I have talked more of politics,
> fairness, and political philosophy than is customary at
> such conferences.  That is because I think that,
> however limited my own perceptions of such

12

considerations, these are precisely the concerns that the debate ought to be about.  Even assuming that the AVF is sufficient in numbers and quality to be an effective military force - and there is, as noted, reason for serious doubt about that over the long term - and recognizing that it is a hopeless system for raising troops in time of emergency or war, the issue is one of social policy and morality and what citizens owe for the benefits they receive in the most widely civilized state that the world has ever seen.[16]

## CONCLUSION

It seems clear to me that a case can be made that supports why the United States does not use the draft during peace to meet its armed forces manpower needs.  Recruiting is working well. The idea of involuntary servitude of only a very small portion of the population is not palatable to the American people.  With the exception of the two world wars, the United States has never really needed the draft to meet manpower objectives (i.e. the draft was chosen over other options available).

It is also true that the use of the stand-by draft is needed to meet a large build-up for emergencies or sustainment of the armed forces when protracted or total war conditions exist.

However, accepting these traditional beliefs denies the nation legitimate and necessary capabilities to better manage accessions in the uncertain era we are entering.  The traditional draft could be modified to reduce those aspects which have historically made it unpopular while still providing utility to the national security goals.  Mr. Kester is correct in proposing the use of the draft during periods of peace as well as war.

13

First, the inequities must be fixed.  Then the following benefits could accrue to the nation:

O   The personnel systems would have some redundancy.  Today, there is total dependence on recruiting volunteers.  There is no back-up system in operation.

O   The armed forces would be operating the manning systems in peace that will be needed in war.

O   There would be a method of supplementing critical skill shortages which recruiting efforts cannot fill.

O   Using the draft would be a signal of national resolve to our Allies.

O   The general population would be involved in the military experience - albeit to a limited degree.

## ENDNOTES

1.   Thomas Gates, Chairman, <u>President's Commission on an All-Volunteer Armed Force,</u> p. 9 (hereafter referred to as the Gates Commission).

2.   <u>Ibid.,</u> p. 10.

3.   David P. Handel, LTC, <u>The Selective Service System: A Historical Perspective,</u> p. 54.

4.   <u>Army Pamphlet No. 20-212,</u> p. 15.

5.   Handel, p. 55.

6.   <u>Ibid.,</u> pp. 27-29.

7.   <u>Ibid.,</u> pp. 31-33.

8.   Gates Commission, p. 124.

9.   <u>Ibid.,</u> p. 123.

10.  Richard Halloran, <u>Serving America: Prospect for the Volunteer Force,</u> p 18.

11.  <u>Ibid.</u>, pp. 23-33.

12.  <u>Ibid.</u>, p. 27.

13.  John G. Kester is an attorney and a frequent writer on defense, government organizations, public policy, and politics. From 1969-1972, he served as Deputy Assistant Secretary of the Army (Manpower and Reserve Affairs) and from 1977-1980 as the Special Assistant to the Secretary of Defense.  He has been a member of the Board of Advisors of the U.S. Air Force Academy and of the Academic Advisory Board of the U.S. Naval Academy.

14.  John G. Kester, "The Reason to Draft," in <u>The All-Volunteer Force After a Decade,</u> ed. by William Bowman, Roger Little and G. Thomas Sicilia, p. 302-303.

15.  <u>Ibid.</u>, pp. 304-306.

16.  <u>Ibid.</u>, p. 312.

## CHAPTER THREE


## RECRUITING AN ALL-VOLUNTEER FORCE


> ...Because the volunteer force has been proven to be highly effective and we have demonstrated the ability to attract the number of people we will need during the next decade, there is no need for either a peacetime draft or national service to satisfy military requirements. There is, however, a strong need to sustain our success by maintaining the purchasing power and competitive appeal of recruiting/retention resources, incentives and compensation...We cannot afford to bid up the price for military manpower by setting up competitive forms of service.[1]

The Gates Commission was the vehicle which launched the United States' pursuit of maintaining a sizable standing army during a period of high threat, yet relative peace, through the accession of an all-volunteer force. As has already been shown, this was a significant departure, both historically and procedurally, from patterns of the recent past. Small standing armies, militia, and the use of the draft were the norms. So it was with uncertainty and with a great deal of anxiety that the nation moved into a new era of providing the manpower to meet national security objectives.


## BACKGROUND


The All-Volunteer Force (AVF) concept experienced difficulties in the decade following the suspension of the draft in 1973. As a result, the U.S. Army began the decade of the eighties in serious trouble. The Army was failing in its efforts to sustain a viable force using the All-Volunteer Force concept.

In 1980, only 54% of new recruits were high school graduates, while in the general population 74% of eighteen through twenty-three-year-olds were high school graduates.[2] Although end strengths were generally reached during the first decade of the AVF, with the exception of a Department of Defense shortfall of 25,000 in 1979, success was attributed to the post-Vietnam strength reductions rather than an effective recruiting program.[3] During this same period, the quality of recruits entering the services dropped significantly when measured against entrance testing levels, attrition during initial enlistment, and percentage of new accessions with high school diplomas.

Another contributing factor to the lower quality of recruit was the incorrect norming of the examination used to measure new soldiers' aptitudes. This resulted in all of the armed forces unwittingly accepting a higher percentage of Mental Category Group IV than intended. Congress had restricted each service to a ceiling of 20% of the total number recruited to fall in Mental Category Group IV. During the five year period of inaccurate testing (1976-1980), the Department of Defense level of Group IV rose to 25% and the Army level exceeded 45%.[4] By 1980, the issue raised during the Gates Commission concerning the percentage of blacks in the armed forces also became a reality with black youth comprising 30% of the total accessions in 1980. The population base of the same age group of blacks was 13% in the United States.[5]

17

By the end of the first post draft decade (1983), all of the negative trends began to reverse. Turnover rates declined from an average of 22% during the period FY 1974-1977 to less than 18% in 1983. By 1983, nearly 90% of recruits were high school diploma graduates compared more favorably with the national population average of 72% high school graduates. When the accession test was properly normed, the Army was able to raise Mental Category Groups I - III accessions to 88% in 1983. Additionally, the proportional representation of black recruits had begun a down turn to 23% of the total enlistees.[6]

The year 1983 was the turn around year for the AVF. For the Army, high school graduate recruits reached 91%, recruits who scored in the top three mental categories reached 96%, and blacks as a percentage of the enlistees and as a percentage of the nations population adjusted to a rate of 19% and 15% respectively.[7] These positive trends continued during the period 1984 to 1989. The 80's closed out with the Army declaring the All-Volunteer Force a success - even with a strong economy at work and a youth population size getting smaller.

## ASSESSMENT

By all analytical indicators, the Army today is in great condition. This is validated by the perception of the civilian and military leaders in the government and by accounts of officers, non-commissioned officers and soldiers in the Army. The Army is better than it has ever been in our nation's history.

The soldiers are smarter, better motivated, easier to train, and more disciplined than ever before.[8]

There are a number of factors that have made the all-volunteer force successful. The most succinct presentation is included in a work by General Maxwell Thurman in The All-Volunteer Force After a Decade.[9] General Thurman has served as the Commander of the U.S. Army Recruiting Command, the Deputy Chief of Staff for Personnel, the Commander of the Training and Doctrine Command, and he is currently a war fighting Commander-in-Chief in Southern Command. These positions have provided him a unique perspective from which to assess the AVF. As the commander of the recruiting force, General Thurman was the architect of the turnaround discussed earlier in this chapter.

The success factors he suggests are:

**ECONOMICS.** The Gates Commission correctly identified the need for better pay to attract and retain a quality force. While initial pay adjustments were made at the time of the abolishment of the draft, comparability was not sustained through the seventies. Once pay was adjusted, strength and quality trends began to improve. Coupled with pay, Thurman attributes a smarter use of bonuses and incentives (like education), improvements in market analysis, better advertising techniques, and progress in the training of the recruiting force as cornerstones for a more effective use of accession dollars. In summation he says, "...we have a better understanding of the supply of available youth, the recruiting environment, and the use of recruiting resources."[10]

Another dimension of economics is the relative cost of recruiting an AVF. The Gates Commission concluded the AVF would be more expensive than the drafted force because of the higher wages required for the volunteers. As recruiting techniques improved, critics observed that the costs of a large recruiting force, advertising costs and incentives costs would all contribute to an unaffordable AVF. The budget for FY 1989 was $645 million. The force recruited was 115,000 with the average cost per accession of approximately $5,600 each.[11]

Recent studies show, surprisingly, that the cost of recruiting volunteers is less expensive than drafting a force would be. A March 1988 General Accounting Office study concluded that a draft force would cost $2.6 billion more per year than a recruited force (1978 dollars).[12]

PEOPLE. In the early years of recruiting an AVF, the Army had to learn about people. The supply of people is not unlimited; it is a finite number, and not all people want to serve in any of the armed forces. Ohio State University conducted research that revealed that only 27% of the seventeen-to nineteen-year-old male high school graduates had any interest in military service.[13] Understanding of the motivators for youth to serve enabled the Army to better focus its recruiting efforts and to attract high quality, college-bound youth. This helped identify the incentives required to recruit and enabled identification of resources that would attract that population to service in the Army.

An additional factor, essentially ignored by the Gates Commission and the armed services during the early years of the AVF, was the career force. As a result, the heart of the NCO Corps left in large numbers, taking their knowledge and experience with them and leaving a significant void in leadership. New soldiers need to be provided the technical and tactical level of leadership that only the NCO corps can provide. **PURPOSE.** To be successful in the long term, the armed forces had to appeal to youth with more than just competitive wages. This factor addresses "Be all you can be." Appeals to youth became: come to the Army for training, education opportunties, fulfillment, and service to your country. The focus for the Army shifted to experiencing the use of high tech equipment and sharing the adventure of demanding training.

## THE OPPOSITION

In June 1986, The Congressional Budget Office conducted a study on the cost of manning the active Army. The report cites the high standards the Army has for recruits and asks if the Army really needs a force that is of higher quality than the general population from which it is drawn. The conclusion of the study was that the Army should reassess how much it can afford to spend in a period when all defense costs may have to be cut.

These 1986 observations are very germane to 1990. The President's 1991 Budget proposes significant reductions in the size of the Army over the next five years and severe dollar decrements.  While some will argue that the drive to a smaller force demands an even higher quality of recruit, the question of monies to sustain the recruiting forces has yet to be resolved.

Given that the Army has shown an ability to recruit quality soldiers in sufficient quantities to meet manpower objectives, some critize the AVF's inability to recruit a true cross section of the nation's youth.  It is a fact that 19% of those who enlist are black; a racially balanced draft would limit that percentage to 15%.

Opponents also charge that the armed forces have the opportunity, if not the responsibility, to teach young Americans civic obligation.  Advocates of the national service corps and of the draft cite this as a major feature for randomly selecting a greater cross section for duty in the defense of the nation.

The final criticism of AVF, and perhaps the one with the greatest substance, is that the need to mobilize quickly cannot be met through recruiting volunteers.  The draft will be needed and should be ready to implement immediately.

## CONCLUSION

Recruiting an all-volunteer force to meet the national defense and security requirements has been successful.  Much has been learned by the Army about how to recruit effectively and efficiently during the past seventeen years.  Proof is readily visible in the result of the December 1989 "Operation Just Cause" in Panama.  The soldiers of the United States Army performed their mission superbly.  It can only be concluded that they were able to do so because they were recruited from the best and the brightest individuals that America had to offer - not taken from a random selection of conscripts who might not want to serve in the first place.

Having made that point, there must be serious concerns about the ability of the recruiting system to respond to a future Army that may under-go repeated fluctuations in force structure and size over short periods of time.  The capabilities and limits of the recruiting system must be carefully defined.  There needs to be more planning, preparation, and practice to ensure responsiveness when full mobilization is needed.

## ENDNOTES

1.  Dick Chaney, 7 July 1989 Letter to the Director of the Office of Management and Budget.

2.  Lawrence J. Korb, "Military Manpower Training Achievements and Challenges for the 1980's," in The All-Volunteer Force After a Decade, p. 7.

3.  Gary Nelson, "The Supply and Quality of First-Term Enlistees Under the All-Volunteer Force," in The All-Volunteer Force After a Decade, p 26.

4.  Ibid., p 32.

5.  Ibid., p 35.

6.  Ibid., pp 25-35.

7.  Richard Halloran, Serving America: Prospect for the Volunteer Force, p 60.

8.  Ibid., pp 15-17.

9.  Maxwell Thurman, "Sustaining the All-Volunteer Force 1983-1992: The Second Decade," in _The All-Volunteer Force After a Decade,_ pp. 266-285.

10.  _Ibid.,_ p. 274.

11.  The detailed costs of recruiting for FY 89 was: a) recruit 115,000; b) operate 2000 recruiting stations; c) $400M -payroll and overhead of USAREC; d) $95M - Advertising; e) $150M -Incentives. (Source: PA&E, HQ, USAREC)

12.  Holloran, pp. 49-57.

13.  Thurman, p. 274.

CHAPTER FOUR

NATIONAL SERVICE

The "manning the force" paradigm has been simple - recruit
volunteers or use the draft.

The "manning" paradigm is now being challenged.  Eight
separate bills have been introduced for consideration by the
101st Congress which could result in a dramatic change in the way
we man the force.  These bills propose a national service concept
aimed at finding ways of involving America's young people in
voluntary service activities.  Several of the bills include
voluntary military service as one of their dimensions.  The
Citizenship and National Service Act of 1989 (S.3) by Senator
Nunn and four others, and H.R. 660, which is identical to S.3, by
Representative McCurdy and twelve others, were introduced in
January 1989 and have moved the issue of national service and its
effect on the military to the forefront.

This chapter addresses the Nunn-McCurdy Bill and provides an
assessment of its potential impact on the U.S. Army.

BACKGROUND

The purpose of the Nunn-McCurdy Act is to renew the ethic of
civic obligation and to spread the responsibilities of
citizenship more equitably.  It provides opportunities for young
people to pursue education and to purchase affordable housing.

The Act focuses on mobilizing young people and senior citizens to deal with pressing social issues through voluntary service. It also proposes strengthening national defense by encouraging young people to volunteer, making the armed forces more representative of the country at large and assisting the armed forces in meeting personnel accession goals.

The concept of the proposed national service is a non-mandatory, comprehensive program providing for one or two years of volunteer service as a civilian, or two years of voluntary military service. In return, volunteers would receive vouchers for $10,000 for one year service, $20,000 for two years service or $24,000 for military service. These vouchers could be used for higher education, vocational training, or down payments for housing. A $12,000 voucher could be earned for eight years of service in the Reserves.

The volunteers would work at subsistence wages ($100 per week) as civilians or at 2/3 pay and allowances as military.

Eligibility would require U.S. citizenship, a high school diploma or equivalent, and age limits of 17 - 26. Eligibility for military service would include additional criteria as determined by the Secretary of Defense.

Military participants would not be entitled to current veteran education or housing benefits. Two years after the passage of the legislation, all existing federal educational loans, loan guarantees, and grants would be phased out.

Finally, all vouchers would be tax free and valid up to ten years after completion of service.

# ASSESSMENT

The objective of the Army's manning system must be to build and maintain a ready Army, prepared to fight and to win. The Army is currently a quality force which is effective in its roles and missions, representative of society, and adequately resourced by OSD and Congress to maintain a competitive edge in recruiting.[1] In an effort to sustain this quality force, the Army has developed a set of principles and rules that provide a framework to evaluate proposals for national service, including national military service. These principles are articulated in an April 1989 Information Paper published by the Office of the Deputy Chief of Staff for Personnel, and include:[2]

O  **Strategic Principles**, which focus on:

- Achieving comparable force effectiveness.

- Continued competitive edge in recruiting by the Army over the other services and the civilian volunteer agencies.

- Ensuring comparable demographic representation in the force.

- Maintaining a quality force for the same costs.

O  **Operational Principles**, where:

- Military capability is highest priority.

- Quality and discipline of the force must remain high.

- Total accessions must support end strength and readiness.

- Skills and length of service must support needs.

- Pool of first term soldiers must be sufficient to provide a base for future NCO corps.

The conclusions presented in the Information Paper are that for a national service program to be acceptable it must ensure that the competitive edge between the Army and the civilian portion of the national service and between the Army and the other military services must be maintained. Current incentive programs have been mandated solely for the Army (e.g., Army College Fund). The Army believes that these must continue. Additionally, Army incentives must be sufficient to offset the rigors, the risks, and the hardships of duty as a soldier and provide equal pay for comparable work within the Army.

The Army believes that the national service plan must provide for the attainment of comparable demographic representation by race and by gender. It also believes that the plan should be cost neutral. This means that the cost of maintaining the quality force should not be more under the plan than it was before the plan.

So, how does Nunn - McCurdy stack-up? Accepting the Army's principles and rules as valid, S.3/H.R. 660 will need modification before it can be seen as a good idea for the Army.

There needs to be a bigger differential between the benefits of civilian service and the benefits of military service. This can be achieved by paying soldiers serving under military national service full pay and allowances, and eliminating the two year civilian service option which would limit the voucher for civilian service to $10,000. This would increase the differential from $4,000 to $14,000 between civilian and military service.

Also, current Army enlistment incentives must not be jeopardized. The three year, $27,000 Montgomery G I Bill (MGIB), the four year, $36,000 (MGIB), the five and six year enlistment bonuses of up to $12,000 and the Army College Fund, all target high school graduates and collectively draw 60,000 enlistees annually. The ability to fill critical MOS's with mental category I-IIIA is an important readiness issue.

On the surface, the Nunn-McCurdy Bill seems to put the Army readiness, the quality of the force, and the cost of sustainment at risk. The Army position is to test the concept of military national service, using a cautious phased approach, only after adoption of the modifications proposed are included.

## A COUNTER VIEW

Dr. Charles C. Moskos, Professor of Sociology at Northwestern University and past S.L.A. Marshall Chair at the Army Research Institute, disagrees with the Army's position. In his book A Call to Civic Service and his September 1989 paper presented to the Hoover Institution on National Service, Dr. Moskos challenges each of the Army's primary objections of Nunn-McCurdy.[3]

First, Moskos offers survey data that suggests half of all males and one-third of all females would choose the military option for national service. Only 10% would choose civilian service, and the rest would choose not to serve in any capacity. Thus, Nunn-McCurdy should not adversely affect recruiting.

Second, training costs are not driven up by the increased number of two year enlistees. On the contrary, when reserve component training is included in the computation, Moskos contends the costs are driven down and the quality of the reserve components goes up.

Finally, lower pay for military national service soldiers will not cause discontentment in the ranks according to Dr. Moskos. If the lower paid soldier does feel disadvantaged, he could join the regular force. Also, it must be noted that every NATO army, except the U.S., has a two-tracked pay system, and these nations have experienced no ill effects.

## CONCLUSION

In my opinion, both the U.S. Army and the supporters of a national service program have more work to do before either side is ready to move forward. Both sides have considerable merit, however both show incomplete analysis. As the debate continues and the analysis progresses, two key factors should remain at the top of everyone's list:

O The idea of national service is a good idea. Involving Americans on an equitable, voluntary basis in activities for the good of the country builds character in the volunteers and in the nation.

O The sustainment of a high quality, ready force is vital to national interest.

The concept of a national service program should not be held hostage by the difficulties of the military service dimension of the proposal. Nor should the national defense capabilities be put at risk by a national service proposal that senior military leaders have serious reservations about. The legislation should be modified to introduce national service in phases - the civilian service component, followed by the military component after testing and further refinements. Concurrently, military leaders must guard against the tendency to dismiss new ideas simply because they are new or because they are a change from the status-quo. This tendency was evident in the Department of the Army and Department of Defense staff papers reviewed for this analysis. Future manning challenges may not be so easily solved with traditional methods. Openness to compromise by both Congress and the military could result in the refinement of the national service proposal into an accession process which is ideally suited for meeting military manpower needs.

## ENDNOTES

1. Allen K. Ono, LTG, Army Position on National Service -ACTION MEMORANDUM, Memorandum to the Chief of Staff, Army, 25 April 1989.

2. Ibid.

3. Charles C Moskos, National Service and Its Enemies, pp. 15-16.

# CHAPTER FIVE

## CONCLUSIONS AND RECOMMENDATIONS

The United States is an acclaimed world power. With this title comes international responsibilities. Perhaps the first responsibility is to accept the role of a world leader, which may also be the most difficult. What the U.S. thinks and what it does has ramifications throughout the world. It seems, therefore, that we, as a nation, must ensure protection of our capability to project power in an influential way.

Power is projected in a number of ways: economical, political, social/psychological, and military. There is growing concern that our economic position as a world leader is declining. Efforts are underway to fix this deficiency. This is vital because effective projection of power is based on the composite strength of a nation to project strength in each area.

The Department of Defense represents the arm of government that provides the U.S. capability to project military power. The changing situation in Eastern Europe does not diminish the need for retention of the military element of power. On the contrary, changes in this region can be seen as more destabilizing than stabilizing. This, coupled with regional and global terrorism, the drug crisis, and the proliferation of sophisticated weapons to potentially hostile nations, further justifies keeping a strong military capability.

I am not arguing for the sustainment of the Army at a strength of 780,000. Rather, I am arguing for the necessity to maintain a capable Army that is able to meet its mission of projecting military power throughout the world where vital U.S. interests exist.

To achieve this goal, LTG Ono is absolutely correct in his assessment of the need for a long range personnel plan which gives the Army the ability to reduce or expand while maintaining readiness. To achieve this goal, a dynamic personnel accession system is needed. The current recruiting system is working very well. That is not the issue. The issue is how to achieve the flexible response ability asked for by the DCSPER in the future.

I recommend:

1. The U.S Army Recruiting Command needs to determine its marginal "costs of doing business." By this I mean an analysis of the upper and lower ends of mission capability. This analysis should relate the accession mission to the organizational size, budget, and time constraints. As previously stated, it costs $5,000 per recruit with the current structure and resources. The analysis will provide an objective look at the cost of recruiting incrementally (either a greater or smaller mission). The analysis can also show how quickly USAREC can recruit if the force needs to expand rapidly. USAREC has constraints. Completion of this analysis will enable the Army to develop contingency plans.

2. Once the outer bounds of the volunteer recruiting capability are known, wedge in alternative accession systems to

support or supplement in the specific deficient areas.  A redesigned draft, as outlined in Chapter 2, could be put in place to supplement the recruiting effort.  Specifically, a draft call could be used to fill critically short skills when such shortages are determined to put mission capability at risk.  A secondary effect is that the use of the draft would allow that system to be exercised.  The nation and the Army do best in war those things that are rehearsed and practiced in peace.

Another wedge that should be worked into the accession system is the option of national service.  Perhaps the congressional proposal holds the most potential for a long range solution to providing a _flexible_ accession system.  Properly modified, the national service legislation can provide the nation the advantages of a public service system while providing to the Defense Department control over the quality and quantity recruiting concerns.  This system can also offer great flexibility without resorting to the general unpopularity that results from the use of the draft.

3.  Finally, I believe more openness to possible alternatives to traditional ways is needed by senior personnel planners.  This openness may have the pragmatic effect of better aligning Army objectives with those in government who control the resources.  I am not promoting the support of bad ideas.  I am promoting a more _objective_ evaluation of all options.  Frequently, new ideas do not receive fair evaluation because they are subjected to the "...if it is not broken, don't fix it." theory.  Many Army leaders believe the current recruiting system

is working great.  Therefore, they conclude, proposals like national service should be rejected.

There is only one issue where there can be no compromise. The U.S. Army must always be ready to perform its mission to keep America free and protect her vital interests.  A more flexible personnel accession system will enhance that ability.

# OPERATING PRINCIPLES OF REDUCTION AND EXPANSION

## REDUCE

1. MAINTAIN READINESS

2. MAINTAIN QUALITY

- RECRUITING CONTINUES

- RETENTION IS SELECTIVE

- REDUCE ON ARMY'S QUALITY TERMS

- CONTINUE DEVELOPMENT, ASSIGNMENTS, ADVANCEMENT AND QOL AT TODAY'S STANDARDS

## EXPAND

1. MAINTAIN READINESS

2. MAINTAIN QUALITY

- RECRUITING EXPANDS

- RETENTION IS SELECTIVE

- EXPAND IN ARMY'S QUALITY TERMS

- PROVIDE DEVELOPMENT, ASSIGNMENTS, ADVANCEMENT AND QOL AT TODAY'S STANDARD

# OPERATING PRINCIPLES OF REDUCTION AND EXPANSION

CONTINUED

## REDUCE

### 3. BALANCED AND ORDERLY

○ MAINTAIN ACCESSION FLOW

○ CUT MID AND SENIOR PEOPLE

○ RETAIN EXPANSION BASE

### 4. RETAIN THE BEST

○ USE BOARDS TO REDUCE

○ CONTINUE PROMOTIONS, SCHOOLS, AND COMMAND SELECTION

## EXPAND

### 3. BALANCED AND ORDERLY

○ INCREASED ACCESSIONS

○ OFFER RECALL TO MID AND SENIOR PEOPLE

○ EXPAND OCS AND NCOES

### 4. BUILD ON THE BEST

○ USE BOARDS TO OFFER RECALL

○ EXPAND PROMOTIONS, SCHOOLS, COMMAND OPPORTUNITIES

# OPERATING PRINCIPLES OF
# REDUCTION AND EXPANSION

CONTINUED

## REDUCE

### 5. RELY ON RESERVE COMPONENTS

○ TRANSITION RELEASED SOLDIERS TO TPU

○ KEEP IRR INVOLVED THROUGH AFFILIATION

### 6. COMPREHENSIVE PLAN

○ UNDERSTOOD BY ALL
○ ELIMINATE UNCERTAINTY
○ PROTECT QOL AND RETENTION

## EXPAND

### 5. RELY ON RESERVE COMPONENTS

○ OFFER RECALL TO IRR AND FORMER ACTIVE DUTY PERSONNEL

### 6. COMPREHENSIVE PLAN

○ UNDERSTOOD BY ALL
○ ELIMINATE UNCERTAINTY
○ PROTECT QOL AND RETENTION

# BIBLIOGRAPHY

1. The Advocates. <u>National service.</u> Debate. Boston: Kennedy School of Government at Harvaed University and WGBH TV, 28 March 1979.

2. Association of the United States Army, Special Report, <u>Is National Service Really Feasible?</u> Arlington: AUSA, 1987.

3. Bowman, William; Little, Roger; and Sicilia, G. Thomas., ed. <u>The All-Volunteer Force After a Decade.</u> Washington: Pergamon-Brassey's, 1986.

4. Brown, James; Collins, Michael J.; and Margiotta, Franklin D., ed. <u>Changing U.S. Military Manpower Realities.</u> Boulder: Westview Press, 1983. Pp. 235-256: "The Citizen-Soldier and National Service," by Morris Janowitz.

5. Chambers, John Whiteclay. <u>To Raise an Army.</u> New York: Macmillan, 1987.

6. Chaney, Dick. The Secretary of Defense, Letter to Director, Office of Management and Budget, 7 July 1989.

7. Coffey, Kenneth J. <u>Manpower for Military Mobilization.</u> Washington DC: American Enterprise Institute, 1978.

8. Committee for Economic Developement. <u>Military Manpower and National Security.</u> New York: February 1972.

9. Daly, John Charles., et al. <u>How Should the U.S. Meet Its Military Manpower Needs?</u> AEI Forums. Washington DC: 6 March 1980.

10. Danzig, Richard, and Szanton, Peter. <u>National Service: What Would It Mean?</u> Lexington: D. C. Heath, 1986.

11. "Does America Need an Army?" <u>U.S. News & World Report.</u> Vol. 107, 11 December 1989, Pp. 22-29.

12. Eberly, Donald J., editor. <u>National Servicee; A Report of a Conference.</u> New York: Russell Sage Foundation, 1968.

13. Gates, Thomas, Chairman. <u>Report of the President's Commission on an All-Volunteer Armed Force.</u> Washington DC: Government Printing Office, February 1970.

14. Goldrich, Robert L. <u>Recruiting, Retention, and Quality in the All-Volunteer Force.</u> Congressional Research Service Report No. 81-106F. Washington DC: Government Printing Office, 8 June 1981.

15.   Halloran, Richard. <u>Serving America: Prospects for the Volunteer Force.</u> New York: Priority Press, 1988.

16.   Handel, David P., LTC. <u>The Selective Service System: A Historical Perspective.</u> Research Report. Maxwell AFB: Air University, May 1985.

17.   Lockman, Robert F., and Quester, Aline O. <u>The All Volunteer Force: Outlook for the Eighties and Nineties.</u> Center for Naval Analysis Professional Paper 433. March 1984.

18.   Moskos, Charles C. <u>A Call to Civic Service.</u> New York: Macmillan, 1988.

19.   Moskos, Charles C. <u>National Service and Its Enemies.</u> Paper for the Hoover Institution Conference on National Service, Stanford, CA., 8-9 September 1989.

20.   Moskos, Charles C. <u>Public Opinion and the Military Establishment.</u> Beverly Hills: Sage Publications, 1971.

21.   Neiderlehner, L., Office of the General Counsel, U.S. Department of Defense, Letter to Senator Sam Nunn, 11 July 1989.

22.   Ono, Allen K., LTG. <u>Manning the Force Issues.</u> Lecture. Carlisle Barracks: U.S. Army War College, 22 November 1989. (Cited with special permission of LTG Ono.)

23.   Ono, Allen K., LTG. <u>Army Position on National Service -- ACTION MEMORANDUM.</u> Memorandum to the Chief of Staff, Army. 25 April 1989.

24.   Ryan, William F. "Reexpansion Plan Is Neded As Budget Compels Cuts," <u>Army,</u> Vol. 39, December 1989, p. 13.

25.   Scowcroft, Brent., editor. <u>Military Service in the United States.</u> Englewood Cliffss: Prentice-Hall, 1982.

26.   Segal, David R. <u>Recruiting for Uncle Sam.</u> Lawrence: University Press of Kansas, 1989.

27.   Sheler, Jeffery L.; Whitman, David; and Shapiro, Joseph P. "The Push for National Service," <u>U.S. News & World Report,</u> Vol. 106, 13 February 1989.

28.   Vuono, Carl E., General. "Quality Tops Chief's List of Imperatives." <u>Army,</u> Vol 39, December 1989, pp. 45 & 52-54.

29.   U.S. Congress. Congressional Budget Office. <u>Quality Soldiers: Costs of Manning the Active Army.</u> Washington DC: Government Printing Office, June 1986.

30.  U.S. Congress. Senate. <u>Citizenship and National Service Act of 1989 (S.3).</u> 101st Congress, 1st Session, Washington DC: Government Printing Office, 1989.

31.  U.S. Department of the Army, <u>Army Pamphlet No 20-212: History of Military Mobilization in the United States Army: 1775-1945.</u> Washington DC: November 1955.